Self-portrait as Ornithologist

Karen Lloyd

Robin

Winter's craftsman, you build unseen citadels of song
and squander bravura overtures on sycamore leaves falling

like the last of rain. Yours is a small waterfall of sound,
a Lakeland beck pouring over lichen-slow stone.

This music is as much the silence between phrases –
a pause to let in the sound of the wood breathing.

Then here you are, framed in the ash. Each of us registers
the other's presence. You speak one syllable, 'tic,' and fly.

Tell me, where does the boundary between us lie;
the partition you keep hidden amongst the trees?

I fail time after time to enter, and your sweet walls
of song, your flashing ruddy beacon tell me, *keep away.*

Surveying, February

We waited for owls
and named the constellations:
Andromeda, Orion, Cassiopeia
and through the 'scope
watched the Dog Star smoulder.

Caught in the westerly
on the rim of Demmings Moss,
were not the outlandish
blandishments of long-eared owls
but snipe, drumming.
The birds' hollow dispatches travelled
through us as if certainty was suspended
or the Earth had tired of itself
and turned along the spine
of the West Cumberland Fault.

Over Warcop Ranges
the neon memoranda
of tracer bullets passed beneath
sodium flares that bloomed and fell
like uncharted stars
sequenced to the calls
of curlews that came,
urgent and incandescent
over Shap's disputed hills.

Self Portrait as Ornithologist

She was speckled, dressed for spring,
plump breast all dots and dashes
held in my cupping palm,
my cheek against her wing.

When she reached the season
of unstoppable song
I found myself speechless.
She was bolshy and wouldn't stop.
She'd found her own urges by then.

Others followed.
The one with eyes like mascara
that had bled in the rain, stick thin legs,
then one with a crest, feet like claws;
that said it all.

The black one was easy.
He loved raisins, apples, earthworms
and singing after rain on summer evenings.
Missed nothing with that bright, sun-ringed eye.

Letting them all go free, though,
I still can't tell you how I found the catch
or pushed the window wide.

Bullfinch

He came in onto the bookshelf beside the open door
and looked for all the world as if he'd come to call –
a gin perhaps, or ginseng tea and talk,
as if the Porsche was just outside and here he was,
all ruddy big-chest swagger, black face and head,
and proceeded to inspect the room – and me.

For maybe one whole minute he sat and cocked
or turned his head, this way, or that, his twinkling
eye on mine again and yet again until,
bored or with the shock of the new,
on a quiet burr of wings, he flew.

He called again on other days –
usually with the wife in tow,
visiting the sunflower feeder at the window
and with his libertine air, twittered,
spat seeds – and winked.

For weeks, I left a little pile of seeds
on the corner of the shelf, hungry for him to call again.
Sometimes I hear him in the birch tree,
enchanter with his bullfinch love-songs,
soaking up the love.

Pittenweem to St Monans

They take me by surprise, the yellowhammers
singing in the whin above the coastal path
singing
little bit of bread and no cheese
the way they had near Arbroath
when we scrambled the cliffs down to the sand
and followed strung lines of salmon nets
out towards the waves.

Out on the Forth I watch two trawlers
drag in opposite directions
though what I want is a big event –
a pod of dolphins or orcas come to call.
On a slab of rock, penitent cormorants,
waiting for something.
The season's first gannets
proceed above the waves,
distant white chains homing towards Bass Rock.

Omey Island, Connemara

Out there, beyond the causeway sands
and the island's rocky brim,
a squabble of white birds
finds tern-shaped fissures in the gale
above the lip of an incoming tide.

The gale, meanwhile, picks flake-white
flints from the waves and another Atlantic
squall is a parallelogram engineered along the horizon.
Half way across the sands our youngsters lean back
into the gale's unruly arms,
the sea blown in ahead of itself,
two edges of water meeting
like lovers after absence.

On this ragged August day a curlew
flies sentinel across the filling tide,
a second rides slipstream
as if the pair were part of the moon's pull,
the weighing sea. One of them remains,
a phone's pixelated blur,
a ghost bird, going. Always going.

Selfie

The Bronze Age fort of Dun Aonghasa sits
above sea-cliffs on Inish Mhor, Aran Islands

As if waiting for a bus on a city street,
she paints lipstick the colour of a bruise,

examines her face in the mirror
and throws her long black hair

until it falls in the required way
then minutely alters her Buddha pose

where three-hundred fractured feet
below Dun Aonghasa, the waves detonate.

And the light snags her white blouse
and it catches also the vagrant gannet

that sculls the rising thermals and dives,
swallowing itself into the unsurprised sea.

The girl leans back a few degrees, tilts her chin,
offers herself to the God of the phone.

YouTube

We will take our devices to the fields,
press play,
watch lapwings tumble
over scrapes of nests
and hear them irritate the sky,
capitulate to crows,
become specimens of lost archives
on temporary display.

We will take our devices to the woods,
press play,
listen to willow warblers
synthesising caterpillars into song,
their tiny bones an instrument
transmitting continental shift.
We will watch them become pixilated
amongst emergent leaves.

We will take our devices to the sea-cliffs,
press play,
look down onto ledges
where kittiwakes embarked on stiff-winged
flight, buoyant correspondents of oceanic
speculation – Leucothea, white goddess,
sweet-eyed feathered thing sent to save Odysseus
from the chaos of the sea.

We will take our devices to the field,
press play,
because we were not looking at the field,
because the field is an empty repository
and we must remember how the field was filled.
The field meanwhile, is waiting,
waiting while we press rewind,
play again.

Sycamore

Don't talk to me
of wafting in the breeze
the rustle of leaves
or being a self-seeking weed

This is what I am

The running itch of treecreeper
sun-ringed eye of blackbird
rain-pulsed
jay-worn
breathing vertically
breathing motorways of water
the repetition of bringing in
and pumping out

I have no choice
other than to be here
to be solid, rooted
silent brazen
rain-slicked
storm-voiced
storm-lost

broken mended
giving taking
striving for light
the almost not
conversation of birds

Pond Frogs, Lake Prespa

Out in the darkness a female frog crams
her shambolic self into the meeting place
of ground and wall. She is a car wreck of a frog,
legs akimbo like a newborn's unfixed limbs,
her skin awash with dots and dashes,
the twin gun covers of her eyes accommodating
lightning, rain and puddles.

The anti-song of pond frogs is a night-time
flood that travels over the scrub of the island.
Throngs of froggy neurons fire themselves
along rainwater highways among stone houses
and old buildings too busy crumpling
under the great responsibilities
of age and weather.

The frogs are Steve Reich on a three-note bender.
An outbreak, a contamination even, of sex;
if only it were funny...
amphibian desperados with one thing –
and I mean one thing only – on their minds.
Mind, I would kiss one; I would.
I would fasten my lips to his if only
it would lead to blessed sleep.

Meanwhile, above my froggy echo-chamber,
in pantile hovels restless starling mothers
gather their pterodactyl broods
underneath wings of stars.

And the rain falls.

There is no rest for any of us, only this;
the voluptuous syntax of rain, dripping from gutters,
drenching the reed-beds on the lake,
racing herculean races along the trampled pathways
of the goats and the sheep and the shepherd
and his dark-eyed slow wife. Only the rain,
smoothing the infinite overtures of frogs,
oiling the thunderstruck journeys
of these hapless refugees.

Goldfinches
after Hieronymus Bosch

We are the thistle-eaters, gossipmongers
of teasel, weeds and sunflowers.

We come in like gaudy apparitions,
bring our clown-masks to the business

of seed, to the business of the feeders
under the clematis arch, our idiosyncratic

frazzle and spark, the way sunlight
filters through the fans of our wings.

In our dozens, we anoint the silver birch
with quarrel, chatter and chinwag.

But inside The Garden of Earthly Delights,
when you hungered we fed you blackberries

and carried your troubled soul upon our backs
when you were unfeathered, lost and wild.

Song for a Mountain Hare

Grazer of blaeberry, juniper, ling,
bark scyther, hunter gatherer
of tundra, *lepus timidus*
making small mountains of yourselves
on the in-bye – a snowline breaking
the snowline of the pelt of the field
on the white banner of the hill beyond
the gate, where they said you would be.

Sing softly to them,
and they will stay and scrape away the snow
as you walk amongst them,
and indeed, there you were, silver flecked
with woad, hazel and slate.

But what to sing to a mountain hare
when across the glare of Loch Garten,
a pair of golden eagles drift like cursors
aslant ragged snow, hunting?

Timepiece

How well the ox-eye knows the sun.
The lure of every single dawn;
of what it is to be courted by the light.
Face to shining face the daisy feels the pulse,
absorbs the lucid glow. Sensor of the planet's hum.

Nodding roadside anonymity,
you are not menial, but an earth-bound
satellite, acolyte, unfurled each day
to circumnavigate the sky.
Above all, knowing when the season's shift is done.
Let go your seeds; release that cargo of ideas,
your incandescence, and dazzled days.

Loch Leven

And when the two mute swans lift the heavy cargo
of their bodies out of the loch
and walk as if through water
and the black rabbits on the bank run, stop, run,
and lapwings are looping flags of gossip
and the loch is a spangled dress,
compelled by its own reflection
the grey wagtail clatters against
the window of the hide. I wonder
if it wants to come inside to see what it is
that the few of us in here are seeing out there,
and it's then I see the pinkfoots coming in
over the western rim of the loch,
passing in front of the hills
and the flocking blades of the windfarm,
and the geese persist, ragged and battling,
their strange velocity imprinting
a contoured wind-map above the waves.

'Seen with my own eyes'
In the C12th Topographia Hibernia, Bishop Gerald of Wales
described how Irish churchmen would eat the Barnacle Goose
during fasts because they were 'not flesh nor being born
of the flesh'

Ultima Thule – far north enough
to be out of sight, sunk deep in the silent,
icy geology of centuries, old ships
lie broken, rotting – splintered hulls,
timbers un-sprung, masts like drunken
trees under continents of ice.

We have sent our special envoys
to bring back specimens for our inspection.

Put your ear to the frozen surface.
Listen for worms unscrewing
themselves from drowned wood.
Keep watching.

The worms turn, become things of feathers,
white mask, pitch neck and beak, webbed feet;
like marsh geese, but somewhat smaller.

Some said they grew on trees
and being neither fish nor fowl could be eaten
by Bishops and Religious Men on days of fast.

I have frequently seen, with my own eyes,
more than a thousand of these small-bodied birds.

In all this, this jiggery-pokery
of spontaneous life –
Rood Goose, Claik, Barny, Tree Goose –
you become a creature made of magic.
I know this; I see and hear it when you fly.

The Piano in the River

They found you in the gorge
below the bridge
strings pebbled shut

now bluebell-hummed
the chip and chisel water
plucks your tongue

underwater weather-babble
assonant salmon-run stream
play me your variations
hear dragonflies click-sing
extemporising into flight
(exuvia diminuendo)

set to sunlight through new leaves
and over your water-thrummed strings
mayfly spin
to thrush music
to blackbird recitative

the moon's a troubadour
fragmented in the midnight stream

I'm listening still
the ones who threw you in
they couldn't hear you sing

Plums

And how to reach the wanton topmost
in their come-hither, half-hidden clusters
or wait for the inevitable fall
into late summer, long grass
before the great give-away?
A benevolence of plums. A gift. A reckoning.

Picking them last year
the Somerset heat hard grafted onto us
the wasps were all boozy,
and indolent like after sex, asleep in crystal
caves of their own making.

I heft one in the hand as the knife
splits bronze-age skin.
And here's the pit, unburied
from its sweet sarcophagus,
the gold-green syrup in the pan
and later, on my tongue, golden parentheses
haul me sweet and sharp back to my mother's kitchen.

Lignum Vitae

Here, where the river falls
in sinuous curves,
where last winter the Sprint
gifted a twist to the bridge,
tight in the base of a rusting globe
a turned piece of wood
the size of the back of my hand,
the hub on which a turbine rested
and spun and pushed water under pressure
through arteries and veins to power
the machine where cloth was made.
Horse blankets, rough woollens.

What songs these walls have sung
to the rattle and the turn
where the river feels the push from Oak Bank
and everything, everything rests
on a nugget of wood
at the bottom of a rusting globe.

Cleaning up the Neighbourhood

Since the big houses down the road
had the pigeon bloke round
to fix the spikes like anti-tank blockades
along the dormer windows
and the hip-and-valley roofs,
the pigeons have given up the day job,
the early morning calls
of blether, glottal stops and coo.

The slates wiped clean from gigabytes
of accumulated pigeon data.
Inevitable then, that they would end up here,
body-building, pumped with braggadocio,
the females casual, indifferent.
The big oily male getting it on
in the bordello at the bottom
of the garden steps.
Others eavesdropping from gutters,
harvesting information
from collared dove, jackdaw, wren.
The one still wearing his RAF stripes.
The one with the gammy left foot.
Not so much homing
as completely home.

Until that is, the local sparrowhawk
narrows down her search - and hits.

The Moth Problem

We watch my father brandish the rolled-up newspaper,
take aim and thwack it against the wall
under the lightbulb's sallow orbit of the sitting room,
sometimes jumping on the mock-leather sofa
to reach the large brown moth in all its delinquent frazzle.
    My brother and I look on
    as if this were normal behaviour – with regard to moths.

And mum, all thin lips and persecution-complex
is shouting instructions from the corner near the door
    and because it is hot and the window open
    other moths keep coming in to join the party.

But what I hadn't known, was that seen through the magnifying lens
the Clouded Drab, Common Quaker and wondrous Plume Moth
are trimmed with the mink of a Ginger Rodgers gown,
all tawny and luxurious, the stigmata stitched about the wings
the manufacture of aeons,
    though for any moth discovered in our ecosystem,
    time, it seemed, was necessarily short.

Genesis

And on the seventh day, God sat back in his Ikea Poang
chair, lit a cigarette and blew smoke rings that travelled
miraculously in sequence across the skies.
And when the ash tip fell it fell as gritty smuts that set
the ancient Californian forests on fire and all the crews
fought the fires but after weeks of this were too exhausted
to continue. And even when the flames were extinguished,
they flickered like electricity underneath the surface
of the earth, bursting out momentarily in the Mariana trench
before the ocean ate them, then burst out again in Tasmania
where they became the very devil.
And families fled the flames that ate their timber houses
like a Komodo dragon eats a lizard and one particular
family ran to the water and became six bobbing
blonde heads and a dog underneath the jetty
while everything around them burned.

And I do not blame God, even though in Genesis
he tells us that everything is for our use and our use only;
all the fish in the sea and the birds in the sky
and all the creeping things that creepeth along
the ground and the fracking companies and Shell Oil
and the Deepwater Horizon oil spill,
the thousands of sea birds ruined, all the
laughing gulls and the diving gannets and the pelicans
waiting to be cleaned – again – for all the world
like a Pietà; oh, how they are fallen!

Back in the clouds, God begins to hear voices;
they rise into the atmosphere from every corner of the Earth
and some of them speak in tongues and tell us
this is not climate change or the consequences
of our habits upon the planet.
He removes a shred of tobacco from his lip,
considers it for a moment, then stubs out the cigarette
and, vowing to give up again, rises from his chair
and remembers some of the things his mother
taught him, because mothers are the fount
of all knowledge. He goes into the kitchen,
fetches a bucket, some cloths and a Brillo pad.

Wren
after Robert Wilson Lynd

Stitch of a bird, weight of a small coin
nooked and crannied by mossy boulders,
tenant of bark split like riven slate,
from the tip of a fern
you fuel this greening oratory
with song as *brilliant as a rainbow.*

Stumpit-tailed, Tom-in-the-wall
there's nothing of the Jenny
about you; you're too pugnacious,
too much a stub of a bird for that.
A coppiced blur
sustained by moths, caterpillars.

Sing to me of winter.
Of boys got-up in straw and hats
to catch the king of birds
and knot his puffball body to a stick;
Samhain's offer to the close of year.

In the ice months, so many wrens
cram inside a nest-box
that come the spring some of them persist
like fallout shadows.

Little wren you endure;
the tick-tock of you lost inside the holly,
not so much keeping time,
as being.

Acknowledgements:
'Timepiece' and 'Lignum Vitae' were published in *Reliquiae volume 5*,
'The Piano in the River' and 'Goldfinches' were published in
This Place I Know, a new anthology of Cumbrian poetry
(Handstand Press 2018);
'Genesis' was published in *The Essay Daily*.

Cover image: 'Flight Paths' by Mike Barlow

Published by
Wayleave Press,
8 Buoymasters, St George's Quay, Lancaster, LA1 1HL

Printed by:
Andrews, Main Street, Bentham, Lancaster, LA2 7HQ